SOLE PROPRIETORSHIP 101

Registering Your Business in
Jamaica Made Easy

Paula Hagley

Copyright © 2024 Paula Hagley

All rights reserved

No part of this publication may be reproduced in any format, distributed, or introduced or stored in a retrieval system, or transmitted in any form or by any means (electronic, mechanical, photocopy, recording or otherwise) without the prior express written permission of the author/publisher.

In the heart of Jamaica, every small business is a beacon of resilience and the limitless potential of human ambition.

INTRODUCTION

Overview of Sole Proprietorship

A sole proprietorship, also commonly referred to as a sole trader business, is a simple and common form of business structure, particularly used by small business owners and solo entrepreneurs. In Jamaica, this structure is commonly used due to its ease of setup and minimal regulatory requirements. The model is straightforward and costs less to maintain, making it attractive to small-scale entrepreneurs.

Definition

A sole proprietorship is an unincorporated business owned and operated by an individual. The owner is personally responsible for all aspects of the business.

Key Characteristics

a) Simple and inexpensive to establish and operate.
b) Control and decision-making power rests with the

owner.

c) Unlimited personal liability for business debts and obligations.

Importance of Registering a Business

Registering a sole proprietorship provides several legal and financial benefits. It formalizes the business, establishes credibility, makes it easier to access financing and ensures compliance with local laws. An overview of the benefits of registering your business includes:

Access to Financial Services

Business Bank Accounts: Registration allows the opening of a business bank account which is crucial for managing finances.

Loans and Grants: The entrepreneur becomes eligible for various loans, grants and other financing offered by financial institutions and government agencies.

Legal Protection

Formality: Provides legal protection and formal recognition of the business name thereby protecting the brand.

Ability to Enter into Contracts: Legally allows the entrepreneur to enter into contracts and agreements using the business name.

Credibility and Trust
Enhances Credibility: Enhances the credibility and trustworthiness of the business. Customers are more likely to trust and do business with a registered entity.
Professionalism: A registered business presents a more professional image.

CHAPTER 1: UNDERSTANDING SOLE PROPRIETORSHIP IN JAMAICA

Main Characteristics of a Sole Proprietorship

(a) The process is governed by the Registration of Business Names Act.

(b) Registering the business entails the registration of the business name.

(c) Registration is renewable every three years.

(d) The owner receives all profits and is responsible for all debts, losses and liabilities.

Comparison with Other Business Structures

To understand the unique aspects of the sole proprietorship, it's essential to compare it with other common business structures:

Partnerships: Unlike a sole proprietorship, a partnership involves two or more individuals who share ownership and management responsibilities.

Partnerships can provide additional resources and shared risk but may also lead to conflicts among partners.

Corporations: A corporation is a separate legal entity from its owners providing limited liability protection. While corporations offer benefits such as easier access to capital and perpetual existence, they are more complex and expensive to establish and maintain.

Suitability of Sole Proprietorship: Who Should Choose this Business Structure

Choosing the right business structure depends on various factors. A sole proprietorship is generally suitable for:

a) Individuals looking to start a small business with minimal regulatory requirements.
b) Entrepreneurs who prefer complete control over their business operations.
c) Businesses with low risk and limited need for external capital.

CHAPTER 2: STEPS TO REGISTER A SOLE PROPRIETORSHIP

Pre-Registration Steps

Before registering a sole proprietorship, it's important to conduct thorough preparation. Among these essential steps are, understanding the target market and outlining a roadmap for the business.

1. Market Research

Understand the target market, competition, and potential customer base. Several private and government organizations offer business support services that include market intelligence for the local and overseas markets.

2. Business Plan

Develop a detailed business plan outlining the business objectives, strategies, and financial projections. This will be a critical GPS to help structure, run and grow the enterprise and facilitate crucial financing.

Registration Steps
1. Tax Registration Number (TRN)
Obtain a Tax Registration Number (TRN). A TRN is essential for business operations in Jamaica. It is necessary for tax purposes, opening a business bank account and conducting financial and other transactions. It is required to register a business.

Applications for a TRN are made to Tax Administration Jamaica (TAJ). Individuals can apply whether they are resident or non- resident.

Application Process to Apply for TRN
To apply for a TRN, submit the following to the TAJ:
(a) A completed TRN application form (this can be downloaded from the TAJ's website).
(b) A government issued identification which may include a Passport or Driver's Licence. A National/Voter's ID may be used, accompanied by the person's Birth Certificate. If the individual is not in possession of any of these, a passport-sized picture certified by a Justice of the Peace or Notary Public as applicable, and the person's Birth Certificate will be accepted.

(c) A Marriage Certificate or legal evidence of other change of name is required where applicable.
(d) Note that if the application is being made from overseas, the person's ID or other supporting document(s) must be notarized.
(e) The application must be submitted in hardcopy to the TAJ.
(f) Applications are to be submitted to the Taxpayer Registration Centre or any TAJ collectorate.

Further details, especially for overseas applicants may be obtained from the TAJ.

2. Choose a Business Name

The business name chosen should be unique and not misleading. It must not resemble existing business names, be offensive or infringe a registered trademark. Certain words may be restricted or require special approval, for example, names containing the words "Royal", "King" or that may suggest connection with the government. (More information on name choice may be obtained from the Companies Office of Jamaica or an attorney-at-law).

3. Licences and Permits

Additional legal requirements may apply depending on the nature of the business.

Licensing: Certain businesses require specific licenses or permits to operate legally. Check with the relevant local authority to determine if the business falls within this category.

Compliance with Local Laws: Ensure that the business complies with all local regulations, including health and safety standards.

4. Register the Business

Registration of the business essentially entails registering the business name. This is done at the Companies Office of Jamaica (COJ) and includes the following:

(a) Complete the BRF1 Form (Super Form) which may be downloaded from the COJ's website or in-office, and submit together with supporting documents including:
    i. A government issued identification which may include a Driver's Licence, Passport or National ID.
    ii. Proof of address which may be a Driver's Licence, Passport, Utility Bill or Bank Statement.

    iii. Proof of citizenship. Non-CARICOM nationals will need to submit a work permit issued by the Jamaican Government if there is no proof of Jamaican citizenship.

(b) A Certificate of Registration is issued upon successful application. The Registration is renewable every three years

(c) The application may be made online or in person.

Post-Registration Steps

After registering the business, there are several important steps to consider.

1. Open a Business Bank Account

Separate personal and business finances by opening a dedicated business bank account. This is crucial especially to financiers. Most small businesses will require financing at some stage of the Seed, Early Stage or Growth cycle of the business.

2. Set Up an Accounting System

Implement a reliable accounting system to track income, expenses and financial performance. This is critical in helping financiers determine the credit or investment readiness of the business. There are several online, simple, cost-effective accounting software that are useful at the early stage of business. QuickBooks is one such example. Alternatively, outsource to an accountant that caters to small businesses.

3. Hire Employees (if applicable)
If there is a plan to hire employees, ensure the business complies with labour laws and regulations.

CHAPTER 3: BENEFITS OF REGISTERING A SOLE PROPRIETORSHIP

Simplicity and Ease of Formation

Establishing a sole proprietorship is straightforward and involves minimal paperwork and legal formalities compared to other business structures like corporations or partnerships. There are typically fewer bureaucratic hurdles and lower startup costs.

Full Control and Decision-Making Power

As the sole owner, the proprietor has complete control over all business decisions without the need to consult partners or a board of directors. This autonomy can lead to faster decision-making and a more agile business operation.

Direct Access to Profits

The owner receives all the profits generated by the

business, which can be particularly motivating and rewarding. There is no need to share profits with partners or shareholders.

Lower Costs and Regulatory Burden

Operating as a sole proprietorship typically involves lower ongoing costs related to compliance, reporting, and administrative requirements. There are generally fewer regulations and formalities compared to corporations.

Privacy

Sole proprietorships often require less public disclosure of information compared to corporations which need to file detailed annual reports and disclose financial information. This can help maintain a higher level of privacy for the owner.

Flexibility

Sole proprietorships offer flexibility in managing and running the business, allowing the owner to easily make changes to business operations, strategies or products and services offered.

Personal Relationships

Sole proprietorships often allow for closer relationships with customers and clients, fostering a personal touch that can be beneficial for business.

Easy to Dissolve

If the owner decides to cease operations, dissolving a sole proprietorship is typically less complicated and costly than winding down a corporation or partnership.

CHAPTER 4: COSTS INVOLVED

The startup of a sole proprietorship involves minimal initial costs.

Initial Registration Costs
Business Registration: Registration of the business name at the Companies Office of Jamaica attracts a small cost.

Tax Registration Number (TRN) Application: While there is no fee for obtaining a TRN, there may be minimal administrative costs associated with gathering required documentation.

Recurring Costs
Renewal of Business Registration: There is a small cost to renew the registration every three years.

Licensing Fees: Certain businesses require annual licenses or permits which come with associated fees. Note that such fees apply regardless of the legal structure of the business.

Budgeting Tips for New Entrepreneurs

Undercapitalization and issues of financial accountability are some of the challenges faced by smaller businesses. Effective budgeting can mitigate these challenges and help to sustain the business past the seed stage. The following is a useful approach to budgeting:

Create a Detailed Budget: Outline anticipated expenses and revenue.

Monitor Cash Flow: Regularly track income and expenses to determine the overall financial health of the business.

Separate Personal and Business Finances: Keep business and personal finances separate. It provides a much clearer picture of the financial status of the business and helps the business attract financing.

Track Receipts: Keep all receipts, even the small purchases. The seeming minor costs add up.

Non-Essential Items: Isolate non-essential items and try to eliminate them.

Negotiate with Suppliers: Always negotiate with suppliers for better prices and shop around.

Use Freelancers: Try freelancers before hiring staff.

Budget for Loans: Don't neglect to plan ahead for any business loans being carried by the business They won't go away on their own.

Plan for Contingencies: Set aside funds for unexpected expenses or opportunities, they will arise.

Taxes: This may seem obvious but many times doesn't prove to be the reality. It is an expense the business does not want to find out about the hard way.
Don't forget to factor it in.

Business Associations: Join a business association. The power of networking is priceless.

CHAPTER 5: CHALLENGES AND SOLUTIONS

Although a simpler business structure, there are several challenges associated with operating a sole proprietorship. The following outline some of the difficulties:

1. Unlimited Personal Liability
In a sole proprietorship, the owner is personally liable for all business debts and obligations. This means personal assets such as the proprietor's home or savings, can be used to satisfy business debts. The entrepreneur does not have the legal protection that a corporation's limited liability structure provides.

2. Difficulty in Raising Capital
Limited Funding Options: Sole proprietors often have fewer options for raising capital. This leaves them to rely on personal savings or investments from friends and family which often times is not sufficient.
Investor Reluctance: Investors are generally more hesitant to invest in sole proprietorships due to the lack

of formal structure and lesser growth potential compared to corporations.

3. Limited Resources and Expertise
Sole proprietors often have fewer resources at their disposal such as staff, technology, and financial capital, which can limit business growth and efficiency.

4. Market Positioning
The business may face challenges in competing with larger, more established corporations that have greater resources and market presence.

5. Operational Burdens
The business demands significant personal time and effort as the proprietor is often operating solo.

6. Lack of Continuity
A sole proprietorship is tied directly to the owner, in that, the business may cease to exist upon the owner's death or incapacity.

Practical Solutions and Tips
Practical steps can help mitigate some of the inherent challenges of running a sole proprietorship. Here are a few to consider:

1. Unlimited Personal Liability

Form a Limited Liability Company: If the risk becomes too great, consider transitioning to a Limited Liability Company (LTD) to protect personal assets while maintaining operational simplicity.

Insurance: Obtain adequate liability insurance to protect against lawsuits and business risks.

2. Difficulty in Raising Capital

Develop a Solid Business Plan: A well-crafted business plan can attract lenders and investors by demonstrating the potential for profitability and growth.

Explore Alternative Funding: Investigate grants, microloans, crowdfunding, and other financing tailored to small businesses.

Build Strong Relationships: Network with potential investors and financial advisors who can provide funding opportunities and financial guidance.

3. Limited Resources and Expertise

Outsource Tasks: Outsource specific functions like accounting, marketing and IT to professionals or specialist firms.

Use Technology: Leverage software and tools to automate tasks and improve efficiency, such as accounting software, CRM systems, and project management tools.

Mentorship and Training: Join business associations, attend workshops, and seek mentorship from experienced business owners.

4. Market Positioning
Build a Solid Brand: Invest in the brand, such as a high-quality website and consistent marketing materials.
Deliver Exceptional Service: Focus on providing outstanding customer service to build a positive reputation and attract word-of-mouth referrals.
Get Certified: Obtain relevant certifications or accreditations to enhance credibility and trustworthiness.

5. Operational Burdens
Set Boundaries: Prioritize establishing clear work-life boundaries to avoid burnout.
Delegate Tasks: Don't be afraid to delegate as the business grows. Engage contractors or hire staff to handle specific responsibilities.
Join a Business Community: Connect with other small business owners to share experiences and gain support.

6. Lack of Continuity
Create a Succession Plan: Develop a clear plan for transferring ownership and management in the event of incapacity or death.

Train Successors: Identify and train potential successors who can continue the business operations smoothly.

CHAPTER 6: RESOURCES AND SUPPORT

Government Resources

The Jamaican government offers a variety of resources to support small entrepreneurs. By leveraging these resources, small entrepreneurs can gain access to the financial support, training, advisory services and networking opportunities essential for building and sustaining successful businesses. Some of the resources include:

1. Business Support Services

(a) A key government agency responsible for promoting sustainable small businesses, the Jamaica Business Development Corporation (JBDC), offers a comprehensive range of services to support small businesses:

i. *Training Programs:* Workshops and seminars on business management, marketing, financial planning among others.

ii. **Mentorship:** Pairing new entrepreneurs with successful business mentors for guidance and support.

iii. **Business Incubation and Innovation:** Incubation facilities and support for startups to nurture innovation and business ideas.

(b) The Scientific Research Council (SRC) advances research and technology particularly helpful to small businesses. Among its services are:

i. Product Development and Standardization
ii. Food Processing and Manufacturing
iii. Commercialization Support
iv. Testing and Analytical Services
v. Scientific Research

(c) The Bureau of Standards Jamaica (BSJ) plays a central role in driving the competitiveness of Jamaican products and services through quality and standards initiatives. Some of its services include:

i. **Quality Management Systems:** Assisting organizations to implement and certify quality management systems such as ISO 9001.

ii. **Calibration Services:** Ensures the accuracy and

reliability of measuring instruments.

iii. **Laboratory Testing:** Offers comprehensive lab testing services.

iv. **Technical Support:** Helps businesses improve manufacturing processes.

v. **Training and Capacity Building:** Conducts workshops and training on standards, quality management, regulatory requirements and more.

(d) JAMPRO (Jamaica Promotions Corporation) is a primary Governmental resource for business opportunities in export and investments. Some services include:

i. **Market Intelligence:** Market information on local and overseas markets.

ii. **Trade Missions:** Facilitation of businesses in overseas trade shows and trade missions.

iii. **Training:** Facilitates comprehensive training on export procedures and readiness.

2. Grants and Funding Opportunities

Several financing opportunities are spearheaded by the Government to help small businesses succeed some of which include:

i. **Development Bank of Jamaica (DBJ):** Financing tailored to micro, small and medium enterprises (MSMEs), generally through their partners.

ii. **National Export-Import Bank of Jamaica (EXIM Bank)**: Credit solutions for qualified small and medium enterprises (SMEs) involved in certain activities.

Private Sector Support

The private sector is increasingly engaging in offering valuable resources to support small businesses. Among the offerings are:

1. *Business Development Services*

Membership organizations provide advocacy support, training, mentorship and networking. Some organizations to consider are the Jamaica Manufacturers and Exporters Association (JMEA), Small Business Association of Jamaica (SBAJ), the MSME Alliance and the Private Sector Organization of Jamaica (PSOJ).

2. *Chambers of Commerce*

Local chambers of commerce facilitate networking

opportunities and advocate for business-friendly policies.

3. Educational Resources

Entrepreneurial education can provide key insights and perspectives for an aspiring entrepreneur. Resources are increasingly being made available to local entrepreneurs through the formal education system.

Tertiary Courses: Jamaican tertiary institutions offer courses in entrepreneurship applicable to the local small business ecosystem. Consider exploring the following institutions:
(a) University of the West Indies (UWI)
(b) University of Technology (U-Tech)
(c) Northern Caribbean University (NCU)
(d) University College of the Caribbean (UCC)

CHAPTER 7: INCENTIVES MATTER

Importance of Incentives

When applied, incentives can result in lower operational costs thereby improving business profitability. This encourages entrepreneurship and innovation. Incentives are particularly vital for micro, small, and medium-sized enterprises (MSMEs) which often face financial constraints and higher risks. It can enable investments in new technologies, expand operations and improve competitiveness.

A Few Key Incentives

There are several local concessions which may apply to small enterprises. These incentives give relief from duties and taxes such as the Common External Tariff (CET) and the General Consumption Tax (GCT). The CET is a tax applied to imported goods while the GCT is a value-added tax imposed on the supply of local or imported goods and services, above a minimum threshold.

Where to Access Further Information
A complete list of incentives for various sectors, their application and how to qualify, may be obtained from the Ministry of Industry Investment and Commerce (MIIC).

CHAPTER 8: LEVERAGING TRADE AGREEMENTS

Overview of Trade Agreements

Registering a sole proprietorship potentially gives a small business owner preferential access to various international markets facilitated by the country's trade agreements. Jamaica participates in several trade agreements that aim to reduce trade barriers, enhance market access, and promote economic cooperation with other countries.

Understanding these agreements provides valuable insight into how they may expand small businesses beyond the local market.

A Look at Some of Jamaica's Trade Agreements

CARICOM Single Market (CSM)

The Caribbean Community (CARICOM) Single Market (CSM) facilitates duty free access of Jamaican goods into the markets of most CARICOM member states. The CSM potentially offers the following benefits:

Market Access: Jamaican businesses can export goods and services to other CARICOM countries duty free and without facing restrictive trade barriers.

Labour Mobility: Entrepreneurs can employ skilled labour from other CARICOM countries, enhancing their workforce and operational capabilities.

Investment Opportunities: Access to a larger regional market provides opportunities for expansion and collaboration with other businesses within the CARICOM region.

CARICOM Bilateral Trade Agreements
(a) CARICOM/Costa Rica Free Trade Agreement
(b) CARICOM/Dominican Republic Free Trade Agreement

Under CARICOM's bilateral agreements with the Dominican Republic and Costa Rica, many Jamaican goods enjoy duty-free access to these countries.

CARIFORUM/EU Economic Partnership Agreement (EPA)
CARIFORUM comprises the members of CARICOM and the Dominican Republic. CARIFORUM's Agreement with the EU allows Jamaica to export both goods and services duty-free and quota free to the countries of the European Union (EU).

The Commonwealth Caribbean/Canada Trade Agreement (CARIBCAN)
Some Jamaican goods are allowed duty-free access to the Canadian market under this Agreement.

Where to find Further Information
Find detailed information on Jamaica's trade agreements and their benefits, from the Jamaica Trade Board.

How Trade Agreements Benefit a Small Business

Cost Savings: Reduced tariffs and duties lower the cost of exporting goods, making Jamaican products more competitive in international markets.

Market Expansion: Improved access to multiple international markets allows businesses to expand their customer base and increase revenue.

Regulatory Support: Trade agreements often include support mechanisms to help businesses comply with international standards and regulations, reducing the risk of trade barriers.

CHAPTER 9: LIST OF BUSINESS SUPPORT ORGANIZATIONS

From mentorship and funding opportunities to legal advice and marketing strategies, business support services can help small businesses unlock their potential and achieve sustainable success. Where the entrepreneur seeks assistance is largely dependent on the stage of the business life cycle.

The following table represents some of the business support organizations providing services at the different stages of the business life cycle in Jamaica.

ORGANIZATIONS	SEED	EARLY STAGE	GROWTH	MATURITY
Branson Centre of Entrepreneurship	✓	✓		
Caribbean Climate Innovation Centre		✓	✓	✓
Caribbean Mobile Innovation Project	✓	✓		

Organization				
Development Bank of Jamaica (DBJ)	✓	✓	✓	✓
National Export Import Bank of Jamaica (EXIM Bank)		✓	✓	✓
HEART/NSTA	✓	✓		
Jamaica Business Development Corporation (JBDC)	✓	✓	✓	
Jamaica Chamber of Commerce	✓	✓	✓	
Jamaica Manufacturers and Exporters Association (JMEA)		✓	✓	✓
JAMPRO (Jamaica Promotions Corporation)			✓	✓
Jamaica Youth Business Trust	✓			
Joan Duncan School of Entrepreneurship	✓	✓		
KATALYXT	✓	✓		
Morris Entrepreneurship Centre	✓	✓		
MSME Alliance	✓	✓	✓	
Private Sector Organization of Jamaica (PSOJ)			✓	✓
Scientific Research Council (SRC)	✓	✓	✓	✓
Small Business Association of Jamaica (SBAJ)	✓	✓	✓	
Technology Innovation Centre	✓	✓		

1. **Seed Stage** – Also known as the pre-commercialization or proof of concept stage. Viability of the concept is tested.
2. **Early Stage** – Normally characterized by activities such as research and development, marketing, and product development.
3. **Growth Stage** – The business begins to solidify its place in the market, generally makes more money, breaking even or becoming profitable.
4. **Maturity** – The stage of stability and profitability in a viable business.

CONCLUSION

Summary of Key Points

Registering a sole proprietorship involves several steps and important considerations. Here are the key points covered in this guide:

Importance of Registration: Registering a business provides legal protection, enhances credibility, and opens doors to financial services and growth opportunities.

Understanding Sole Proprietorship: A sole proprietorship is a simple and cost-effective business structure, usually used by small-scale entrepreneurs.

Registration Process: Follow the steps to register a business, including pre- registration and post-registration considerations.

Benefits of Sole Proprietorship: Why the model may be attractive to small, startup entrepreneurs.

Costs Involved: The costs associated with the sole proprietorship model. Budgeting tips can help to encourage effective management of the business' finances.

Challenges and Solutions: Understanding common challenges that can face a sole proprietor and apply practical solutions to overcome them.

Resources and Support: Leverage government and private sector resources, as well as educational opportunities to support the business journey.

Incentives: Taking advantage of government incentives can unlock key benefits for a small business.

Trade Agreements: Understanding trade agreements provides valuable insight into how they can expand a small business beyond the local market.

A Guide to Support Services: The local small business ecosystem offers a wealth of services to support small businesses.

Encouragement and Final Tips for Aspiring Entrepreneurs

Starting and running a business is a challenging but potentially rewarding endeavour.

Stay Persistent: Building a successful business takes time and effort. Staying persistent is crucial to taking the business from seed to growth stage and beyond.

Be Adaptable: The business environment is constantly changing. Be open to pivoting and adapting the business strategies and approaches as needed.

Seek Support: Don't hesitate to seek support from mentors, advisors and fellow entrepreneurs. Building a strong support network can make a significant difference.

Focus on Customer Service: Keep the customer at the center of the business. Providing excellent customer service and meeting the customer's needs will drive business success.

APPENDIX
Contact Information for Key Agencies

Companies Office of Jamaica
www.orcjamaica.com; (876) 908-4419
Tax Administration Jamaica (TAJ)
www.jamaicatax.gov.jm; (888) 829-4357
Jamaica Business Development Corporation (JBDC)
www.jbdc.net; (876) 928-5161
Jamaica Manufacturers and Exporters Association
www.jmea.org; (876) 922-8880
Small Business Association of Jamaica
www.sba-jm.org; (876) 927-7071
MSME Alliance
www.themsmealliance.org; (876) 610-9371
JAMPRO (Jamaica Promotions Corporation)
www.dobusinessjamaica.com; (876) 978-7755
Development Bank of Jamaica (DBJ)
www.dbankjm.com; (876) 929-4000
The Trade Board Limited
www.tradeboard.gov.jm; (876) 967-0507
Ministry of Industry, Investment and Commerce
www.miic.gov.jm; (876) 968-7116
Bureau of Standards Jamaica (BSJ)
www.bsj.org.jm; (876) 618-1534
Scientific Research Council (SRC)
www.src.gov.jm; (876) 927-1771

Private Sector Organization of Jamaica (PSOJ)
www.psoj.org; (876) 927-6238
Ministry of Labour and Social Security
www.mlss.gov.jm; (876) 922-9500

www.ingramcontent.com/pod-product-compliance
Lightning Source LLC
Chambersburg PA
CBHW072021230526
45479CB00008B/313